GW00482154

# Jams and Jellies: Preserving By The Pint In Minutes

### Delicious Fresh Preserves You Can Make In Under 30 Minutes With A Jam and Jelly Maker

## Jennifer Williams

Highlands Press

## PUBLISHERS NOTES

Text copyright © Jennifer Williams
Cover, images and text design copyright © Highlands Press

The scanning, copying, uploading and distribution of this book via the
Internet or via any other means without the permission of the publisher is
not permitted. Please purchase only authorized editions, and do not
participate in or encourage electronic piracy of copyrighted materials. Your
support of the author's rights and efforts in the publishing of this book is
appreciated.

**Disclaimer**

This publication is intended to provide helpful and informative material. It
is not intended to diagnose, treat, cure, or prevent any health problem or
condition, nor is intended to replace the advice of a physician. No action
should be taken solely on the contents of this book. Always consult your
physician or qualified health-care professional on any matters regarding
your health and before adopting any suggestions in this book or drawing
inferences from it.

The author and publisher specifically disclaim all responsibility for any
liability, loss or risk, personal or otherwise, which is incurred as a
consequence, directly or indirectly, from the use or application of any
contents of this book.

Any and all product names referenced within this book are the trademarks
of their respective owners. None of these owners have sponsored,
authorized, endorsed, or approved this book. The author is not associated
with Ball®, Jarden Home Brands or Jarden Corporation.

Always read all information provided by the manufacturers' product labels
before using their products. The author and publisher are not responsible
for claims made by manufacturers.

**Paperback Edition**

Manufactured in the United States of America

ISBN-13: 978-0692258118

# TABLE OF CONTENTS

*All recipes use the Ball® FreshTECH Automatic Jam & Jelly Maker to make these delectable no-fuss jams and jellies in under 30 minutes. Get yours here:* www.amzn.to/1p729He

# INTRODUCTION

In all of the cookbooks I have had a passionate desire to develop, making jams, jellies and preserves was not even a twinkle in my eye. I was someone that would always look longingly at all the sumptuous, colorful, glistening berries and fruits at my farmers market and local grocery. I would purchase only so many that we could eat in a short time before they spoiled, but always wished I could extend that mouthwatering experience.

Alongside all the fresh berries and fruits are the endless variety of gourmet jams and preserves that grace the aisles near the cheese and bread and fresh produce. The diversity and interesting flavors that were combined into these preserves was mind blowing. I would always buy a few to try and thus began to expand the flavors I enjoyed. I loved to serve them with cheese as an appetizer, as an addition to sandwiches and often as a glaze on roasts.

While I had contemplated marrying these two desires and making my own preserves, the task seemed rather daunting. I had watched both my grandmother and mother canning and preserving, but that was always using fresh vegetables from the garden and an occasional fruit. I had never seen them make jams, jellies or other preserves.

My grandmother had taught me the basics of canning one summer before I headed back to college. My grandparents were so pleased that they could send something along with me back to school. So my grandfather helped me pick the vegetables from their garden and my grandmother helped me clean, prep and either can or freeze them. The experience is one that I will always cherish and the great part was that I had a school years' worth of homegrown veggies – great for the budget and even better to have great foods I knew were good and always on hand.

The desire to try my hand at making my own preserves persisted. I love trying new recipes and processes and absolutely love eating. And after all, I did have some experience, or so I thought. After looking through countless recipes, I wasn't as sure that this was going to be a good idea. First, I really didn't want to make large batches which seemed to be the most common thread. I guess it makes sense when you have to spend hours boiling, testing and setting up your process that you make large batches to make it worth your while. I also felt intimidated by the 'testing for setting points' and the many things that could go wrong and ruin my scrumptious batch of jam.

What I wanted to do was make small batches, in a short period of time with the fewest possibilities of something going terribly wrong. On one of my searches for a solution, I discovered a Jam and Jelly Maker; a small appliance that promised to make small batches of jams in under 30 minutes and automatically stir my jam or jelly while it cooks, taking the guesswork out of making jams and jellies. Sold!

I started testing my new jam maker with basic recipes that came with the jam and jelly maker such as strawberry and blackberry jams. The process was unbelievably simple. I didn't have to fuss with stirring, testing setting points, skimming foam and toiling over a steamy, boiling pot of jam. The jams came out perfectly. I was done making 4 half pints of jam in under 30 minutes. But I soon realized there was so much more I could do with this handy little machine. First I could test all kinds of other ingredients and in varying combinations. Each batch makes just about 4 of those adorable, decoratively cut little half pint jars of jam. Perfect size for eating in small batches, trying a new recipe and ideal for gift giving. I was very excited!

After trying many different variations of preserves, some inspired by other recipes and some with ingredients I had observed in those gourmet preserves at the store, I came up with numerous easy, inviting and delicious jams and jellies I could enjoy and also give to friends. As I was experimenting with my recipes, I gave small jars to a number of friends and family member to try. I asked for honest evaluations so I could get the best sampling of recipes for this book.

What I wasn't expecting was the almost child-like reactions from people as I gave them freshly preserved jams. I even took some as hostess gifts for dinner parties. The sheer delight that people had from receiving just a couple of jam jars was incredibly rewarding and fun to see. I learned I wasn't the only one that loves to eat these delightful little preserves.

This recipe book is a result of my recipe testing and the wonderful feedback from many people on their favorite jams and jellies. I include many of the traditional, simple recipes such as berry jams and fruit jellies. But I've also expanded the boundaries of jams you can make at home quickly and easily too, such as reduced or no sugar jams, carrot cake jam, Shirley Temple jelly, and preserves made with jalapenos, herbs, scapes and sriracha. Expanding these boundaries gives you so many more options for using jams for appetizers, glazes and in sandwiches and also for specialty gift-giving. With a little bit of ingenuity, you'll find that this clever machine can help you make so many different preserves that you will be able to use in so many ways!

The best part? All of these jams and jellies can be prepared in small batches, in very little time and with less guess work.

Happy jam and jelly making!

Get more information and order your Ball® FreshTECH Automatic Jam and Jelly Maker visit www.amzn.to/1p729He or with your smartphone, scan the code next to the Jam Maker below:

# ACKNOWLEDGMENTS

I cannot even begin to thank the many people that made this book possible without first and foremost giving my heartfelt thanks to my mother. Her endless love and encouragement taught me that you can accomplish anything. Without that, this book would not have been possible.. I wish you were here now to see this book come to life.

To my aunt and godmother Lorraine, who shared many tips on canning and to this day gifts me her amazing canned goods and invites my daughter and me to share in her family holiday celebrations.

My grandma Ida and grandpa John , gave me the appreciation for homegrown and home preserved foods. I so enjoyed romping around their small farm when I was young. When I was heading off to college, they helped me preserve their garden's bounty to get me through some fairly lean years.

My taste testers were many and they rocked. Special thanks to Bryan Ohr, Kris Jenstead, Curt Haugen and my wonderful daughter Natalie for endlessly testing recipes and giving me your valuable feedback, support and encouragement.

# GETTING STARTED

**About the Jam and Jelly Maker**

The Automatic Jam and Jelly Maker is a small kitchen appliance that makes preparing jams and jellies an extremely easy, streamlined process that takes a lot of the guesswork out of making jams and jellies. You just add your ingredients and push a button and the jam maker will automatically heat and stir your ingredients and beep to tell you when your jams or jellies are done.

Once your preserves are done, you spoon them into prepared jars and then you can either freeze, refrigerate or process can your delicious jams and jellies.

The jam and jelly maker makes about 4 half pints of preserves in under 30 minutes. It is a perfect device if you want to make small batches of jams and jellies and reduce the amount of time, effort and potential for problems with your final product.

**Other Handy Tools**

Aside from the jam and jelly maker, there are just a few other kitchen tools that you will need to make your jams and jellies.

*Potato Masher:* To crush your berries and fruits to the right consistency to make perfect preserves, the potato masher is the best tool for the task. Do not use a blender or food processor to crush the ingredients as they will become to smooth.

*Plastic ladle and spatula:* These are used to remove your preserves from the jam and jelly maker. You should only use non-metal utensils so you do not scratch the maker's nonstick cooking surface.

*Funnel for filling canning jars:* A regular and wide mouth canning funnel is needed to fill your jars when removing the jams and jellies from the maker. A narrow necked funnel will not work for this task, so make sure you have a funnel made for canning.

*Canning jars, lids and bands:* Half pint (4 oz) and pint sized (8 oz) jars are ideal sizes for storing your preserves. You can use the glass jars for refrigerating, freezing or fresh preserving. You could also use plastic freezer jars and lids for refrigerating or freezing your jams.

*Labels:* You will want to label all of your jars with the contents and date made. You can use simple labels your can find in office supply stores or decorative labels made specifically for canning jars. If you are going to give them as gifts, you may even want to create your own personalized label.

**The Jam and Jelly Making Pantry**

The beauty of making your own jams and jellies at home is that you can make them exactly the way you like them, using quality ingredients and feel assured that you know everything that went into your jams and jellies. There is an inexplicable satisfaction from making your own fresh preserves and enjoying yourself or giving them as gifts.

## Berries and Fruits

Always use the best produce you can find. The quality of ingredients you put in to your jams and jellies will most certainly determine the quality of your final product. Why go through the time, money and energy if you are not striving for the best you can make. Fully ripened fruits and berries should always be used. Not over-ripe and not under-ripe; either of these will produce inferior results. You will also get the best results by choosing produce that is in season in your area. Not only will the flavor and texture be better, but local in-season berries and fruits often cost less.

## Herbs, Seasonings and Flavorings

When adding fresh or dried herbs, seasonings and flavorings remember that a little goes a long way. Always follow the recommended recipe amounts to make sure you get the correct flavor and consistency. If you are confident in your skills and experience with making these recipes, then you may want to adjust the amounts but do so only in small increments and know that you may get unintended results.

## Sugar

Sugar is used in making jams because it helps in extracting the juices from the fruits and berries, enhancing the flavor and aids in the jelling process which gives the jams a good set. You can also reduce or eliminate the amount of sugar in the recipes if using the right pectin and changing the amount of other ingredients. The recipes in this book will give you many variations for adding sugar. In much of my recipe testing, to my surprise, the hands down favorite was the reduced sugar

(2 cups) jams – this was even with friends and family that have a sweet tooth.

## Pectin

Pectin is a naturally occurring element in fruits and berries. The purpose of pectin is to help the jams set up to the appropriate consistency. The exact amount and type (powdered or liquid) of pectin called for in the recipes should be used. Altering this amount will cause your jams to not set correctly.

In all of my recipes, I used Ball RealFruit Classic Pectin for the traditional and reduced sugar jams and Ball RealFruit Low or No-Sugar-Needed Pectin for the low or no sugar jams. This is a powdered pectin. I especially like that I you can purchase these in 4.7 oz jars, which will give you up to 22 half-pint jars. This flexibility allows me to measure and add just the right amount of pectin for what I want to make.

## Butter

Butter can be added to jams and jellies to reduce foaming. I always add the butter because it reduces one other potential step or issue in making my jams. It is an optional ingredient, but I would highly recommend it. I have never had to skim any excess foam from my jams when using butter in the jam and jelly maker.

## Get Ready, Get Set

Scan the ingredient lists of the recipes that appeal to you to make sure you have everything you need for the jams and jellies you want to prepare. When using fresh berries and fruits, you should purchase them just in time to make your jams and jellies.

You will have the most success with your jams if you prepare all of the ingredients ahead of time and have them ready to go into the jam and jelly maker. Always add the ingredients in the order listed and that is called for in the recipe directions.

Have your jars, lids and rings ready to fill immediately when the jam in done cooking. Wash and sterilize your jars, lids and bands before using. Glass jars should be hot when you are ready to fill them to prevent shattering the glass when filling with hot jam.

**Quick Tips for Perfect Jams and Jellies**

Always use fully ripe fruits and berries. Use the best quality you can find to yield superior results. Wash them and make sure they are dry before using.

Crush your fruits and berries using a potato masher. Do this one layer at a time for the most consistent results. You can experiment with how much or how little you crush your berries. It really depends if you like your jams smoother or with more chunks of fruit. You should know though that during the cooking process your ingredients will break down considerably.

Measure your ingredients carefully to get ideal results. Do not double or reduce the batch size for each recipe since they may not fit or cook correctly in the appliance. Since it only takes 21 to 25 minutes to make a batch, you can easily make more than one batch if you choose.

Stay within earshot of the appliance since you will need to hear the beeping sounds to alert you to add more ingredients or that your jam is done. Failure to follow this timing could result in a ruining your jam.

**Safety Tips**

Cooked jam is extremely hot and can burn you easily. Take care not to touch the jam or handle in such a way that could cause spattering.

The appliance handles can get hot during cooking because of the steam venting out of the cover vents. Use a pot holder when touching the handles, lid or pot.

Once your jams are put in jars and covered, they need to be refrigerated, frozen or process canned immediately. Jams and jellies in this book can be processed using a boiling water canner or a pressure cooker. Use the recommended canning process for your preferred method. You can also serve your jams once they have cooled to a safe temperature and then refrigerate.

**Notes:**

The recipes and instructions in this book are specifically designed to be used with the Ball® FreshTECH Automatic Jam & Jelly Maker , buy it here: www.amzn.to/1p729He , or any other similar Jam & Jelly Maker. The book is not intended to give you extensive canning and preserving instructions. You should consult your local extension service or the USDA Complete Guide to Home Canning. This guide is available for free from the National Center for Home Preservation.

# SECTION 1
# JAMS

# 1
# CLASSIC JAMS

# STRAWBERRY JAM

*Strawberries make a pure and simple jam that so many of us love on just about anything and at any time of the day.*

**PREP TIME:**
2 Minutes

**COOK TIME:**
21 Minutes

**MAKES:**
About 4 (8 oz) half pint jars

### INGREDIENTS

| | |
|---|---|
| 3 tbsp | classic powdered pectin |
| 2 2/3 cups | crushed strawberries (about 3 pounds) |
| 1/2 tsp | butter |
| 3 1/3 cups | granulated sugar |

### DIRECTIONS

1. Pre-measure all ingredients. Set aside.

2. Sprinkle pectin evenly in bottom of jam and jelly maker. Add crushed strawberries evenly on top of pectin. Add butter to top of berries.

3. Press JAM button on maker. The cook time will show 21 minutes. Press enter.

**TIP:**
The berries break down in the jam maker so don't be concerned if your berries have chunks before adding to the jam maker. For a smoother jam, crush your strawberries until chunks are pea-sized.

4. After 4 minutes, you will hear 4 short beeping sounds. Slowly add sugar to top of berries while the stirrer is turning. Cover with glass lid.

5. After 17 more minutes, or until the jam maker beeps again, press cancel on the jam maker and unplug the maker. Carefully remove the glass lid. Remove stirrer using a pot holder.

6. Immediately spoon jam into heated glass jam jars leaving 1/4 in headspace. Cover with lids and rings.

7. Refrigerate up to 3 weeks, freeze up to 1 year, or fresh preserve and store up to 1 year.

# BLACKBERRY JAM

*Blackberries just glisten like royal jewels and make an exceptionally colorful, deeply flavored jam.*

**PREP TIME:**
2 Minutes

**COOK TIME:**
21 Minutes

**MAKES:**
About 4 (8 oz)
half pint jars

**INGREDIENTS**

| | |
|---|---|
| 3 tbsp | classic powdered pectin |
| 2 2/3 cups | crushed blackberries (about 1 1/3 pounds or 4 6-oz containers) |
| 1/2 tsp | butter |
| 3 1/3 cups | granulated sugar |

**DIRECTIONS**

1. Pre-measure all ingredients. Set aside.

2. Sprinkle pectin evenly in bottom of jam and jelly maker. Add crushed blackberries evenly on top of pectin. Add butter to top of berries.

3. Press JAM button on maker. The cook time will show 21 minutes. Press enter.

4. After 4 minutes, you will hear 4 short beeping sounds. Slowly add sugar to top of berries while the stirrer is turning. Cover with glass lid.

**TIP:**
Whenever I make this recipe, I always buy more blackberries. This ensures that I have enough berries for my jam after my daughter and I 'taste-test' the berries.

5. After 17 more minutes, or until the jam maker beeps again, press cancel on the jam maker and unplug the maker. Carefully remove the glass lid. Remove stirrer using a pot holder.

6. Immediately spoon jam into heated glass jars, leaving 1/4 in headspace. Cover with lids and rings.

7. Refrigerate up to 3 weeks, freeze up to 1 year, or fresh preserve and store up to 1 year.

# RASPBERRY JAM

*Red raspberries make a scrumptious colorful jam that is bursting with flavor.*

**PREP TIME:**
2 Minutes

**COOK TIME:**
21 Minutes

**MAKES:**
About 4 (8 oz) half pint jars

### INGREDIENTS

| | |
|---|---|
| 3 tbsp | classic powdered pectin |
| 2 2/3 cups | crushed raspberries (about 1 1/3 pounds or 4 6-oz containers) |
| 1/2 tsp | butter |
| 3 1/3 cups | granulated sugar |

### DIRECTIONS

1. Pre-measure all ingredients. Set aside.

2. Sprinkle pectin evenly in bottom of jam and jelly maker. Add crushed raspberries evenly on top of pectin. Add butter to top of berries.

3. Press JAM button on maker. The cook time will show 21 minutes. Press enter.

**TIP:**
Rinse
raspberries and
let dry
thoroughly.
Lightly roll
raspberries on
a paper towel
before adding
them to the
jam maker to
make sure they
are free of any
extra dirt or
moisture.

4. After 4 minutes, you will hear 4 short beeping sounds. Slowly add sugar to top of berries while the stirrer is turning. Cover with glass lid.

5. After 17 more minutes, or until the jam maker beeps again, press cancel on the jam maker and unplug the maker. Carefully remove the glass lid. Remove stirrer using a pot holder.

6. Immediately spoon jam into heated glass jars, leaving 1/4 in headspace. Cover with lids and rings.

7. Refrigerate up to 3 weeks, freeze up to 1 year, or fresh preserve and store up to 1 year.

# STRAWBERRY KIWI JAM

*The sweet tastes of strawberry and kiwi with a touch of ginger coalesce into a unique, flavor-packed and colorful jam.*

**PREP TIME:**
2 Minutes

**COOK TIME:**
21 Minutes

**MAKES:**
About 4 (8 oz)
half pint jars.

### INGREDIENTS

| | |
|---|---|
| 3 tbsp | classic powdered pectin |
| 2 | kiwi, peeled and diced |
| 2 cups | crushed strawberries (about 2 1/2 pounds) |
| 2 tsp | lemon juice |
| 1 tbsp | minced crystalized ginger |
| 1/2 tsp | butter |
| 2 1/2 cups | granulated sugar |

### DIRECTIONS

1. Pre-measure all ingredients. Set aside.

2. Sprinkle pectin evenly in bottom of jam and jelly maker. Add crushed strawberries, kiwi, lemon juice and ginger evenly on top of pectin. Add butter to top.

**TIP:** You can add more or less sugar depending upon the sweetness you would like. You should keep the sugar measurements in the range from 1 cup up to a maximum of 3 1/3 cups.

3. Press JAM button on maker. The cook time will show 21 minutes. Press enter.

4. After 4 minutes, you will hear 4 short beeping sounds. Slowly add sugar to top of jam mixture while the stirrer is turning. Cover with glass lid.

5. After 17 more minutes, or until the jam maker beeps again, press cancel on the jam maker and unplug the maker. Carefully remove the glass lid. Remove stirrer using a pot holder.

6. Immediately spoon jam into heated glass jars, leaving 1/4 in headspace. Cover with lids and rings.

7. Refrigerate up to 3 weeks, freeze up to 1 year, or fresh preserve and store up to 1 year.

# STRAWBERRY RHUBARB JAM

*The first tastes of the season combine to make a traditional jam that celebrates the beginning of summer.*

**PREP TIME:**
3 Minutes

**COOK TIME:**
21 Minutes

**MAKES:**
About 4 (8 oz) half pint jars.

**INGREDIENTS**

| | |
|---|---|
| 3 tbsp | classic powdered pectin |
| 2 cups | crushed strawberries (about 2 1/2 pounds) |
| 1 1/2 cups | chopped rhubarb |
| 2 tbsp | lemon juice, from bottle |
| 1/2 tsp | butter |
| 3 cups | granulated sugar |

**DIRECTIONS**
1. Pre-measure all ingredients. Set aside.

2. Sprinkle pectin evenly in bottom of jam maker. Add crushed strawberries, chopped rhubarb and lemon juice evenly on top of pectin. Add butter to top.

**TIP:** Fresh rhubarb works best in this recipe. You will need to plan ahead, since rhubarb is not available for very long.

3. Press JAM button on maker. The cook time will show 21 minutes. Press enter.

4. After 4 minutes, you will hear 4 short beeping sounds. Slowly add sugar to top of jam mixture while the stirrer is turning. Cover with glass lid.

5. After 17 more minutes, or until the jam maker beeps again, press cancel on the jam maker and unplug the maker. Carefully remove the glass lid. Remove stirrer using a pot holder.

6. Immediately spoon jam into heated glass jars, leaving 1/4 in headspace. Cover with lids and rings.

7. Refrigerate up to 3 weeks, freeze up to 1 year, or fresh preserve and store up to 1 year.

# BOYSENBERRY JAM

*Boysenberries derive their distinct flavor from their raspberry and blackberry ancestors making an intense, complex flavored jam.*

**PREP TIME:**
2 Minutes

**COOK TIME:**
21 Minutes

**MAKES:**
About 4 (8 oz) half pint jars.

**INGREDIENTS**

| | |
|---|---|
| 3 tbsp | classic powdered pectin |
| 2 2/3 cups | crushed boysenberries |
| 1/2 tsp | butter |
| 3 1/3 cups | granulated sugar |

**DIRECTIONS**

1. Pre-measure all ingredients. Set aside.

2. Sprinkle pectin evenly in bottom of jam and jelly maker. Add crushed boysenberries evenly on top of pectin. Add butter to top.

3. Press JAM button on maker. The cook time will show 21 minutes. Press enter.

4. After 4 minutes, you will hear 4 short beeping sounds. Slowly add sugar to top of jam mixture while the stirrer is turning. Cover with glass lid.

**TIP:**
Boysenberries
are a unique
and rare berry.
They are at
their best when
obtained from
farmer's
markets, farm
stands or
backyard
gardens.

5. After 17 more minutes, or until the jam maker beeps again, press cancel on the jam maker and unplug the maker. Carefully remove the glass lid. Remove stirrer using a pot holder.

6. Immediately spoon jam into heated glass jars, leaving 1/4 in headspace. Cover with lids and rings.

7. Refrigerate up to 3 weeks, freeze up to 1 year, or fresh preserve and store up to 1 year.

# PEACH JAM

*Nothing quite compares to the taste of fresh, juicy peaches – except maybe this richly colored and sweet tasting peach jam.*

**PREP TIME:**
4 Minutes

**COOK TIME:**
21 Minutes

**MAKES:**
About 4 (8 oz)
half pint jars.

**INGREDIENTS**

| | |
|---|---|
| 3 tbsp | classic powdered pectin |
| 2 2/3 cups | pitted, peeled and finely chopped peaches |
| 2 tbsp | lemon juice, from bottle |
| 1/2 tsp | butter |
| 3 1/3 cups | granulated sugar |

**DIRECTIONS**

1. Pre-measure all ingredients. Set aside.

2. Sprinkle pectin evenly in bottom of jam and jelly maker. Add chopped peaches and lemon juice evenly on top of pectin. Add butter to top.

3. Press JAM button on maker. The cook time will show 21 minutes. Press enter.

**TIP:** Choose peaches that give slightly when you gently press your thumb against their skin. You can't tell just by the color of their skin whether they are ripe enough. Wait until your peaches are fully ripe before making this jam.

4. After 4 minutes, you will hear 4 short beeping sounds. Slowly add sugar to top of jam mixture while the stirrer is turning. Cover with glass lid.

5. After 17 more minutes, or until the jam maker beeps again, press cancel on the jam maker and unplug the maker. Carefully remove the glass lid. Remove stirrer using a pot holder.

6. Immediately spoon jam into heated glass jars, leaving 1/4 in headspace. Cover with lids and rings.

7. Refrigerate up to 3 weeks, freeze up to 1 year, or fresh preserve and store up to 1 year.

# PEAR JAM

*The distinctive character, texture and flavor of pears are ideally suited for a jam you can enjoy time and time again.*

**PREP TIME:**
4 Minutes

**COOK TIME:**
21 Minutes

**MAKES:**
About 4 (8 oz) half pint jars.

**INGREDIENTS**

| | |
|---|---|
| 3 tbsp | classic powdered pectin |
| 2 2/3 cups | cored, peeled and finely chopped pears |
| 1/2 tsp | butter |
| 3 1/3 cups | granulated sugar |

**DIRECTIONS**

1. Pre-measure all ingredients. Set aside.

2. Sprinkle pectin evenly in bottom of jam and jelly maker. Add chopped pears evenly on top of pectin. Add butter to top.

3. Press JAM button on maker. The cook time will show 21 minutes. Press enter.

4. After 4 minutes, you will hear 4 short beeping sounds. Slowly add sugar to top of jam mixture while the stirrer is turning. Cover with glass lid.

**Tips:** Anjou or Bartlett pears are particularly nice for this recipe.

Choose pears that have a slight softness near the neck which indicates their ripeness.

5. After 17 more minutes, or until the jam maker beeps again, press cancel on the jam maker and unplug the maker. Carefully remove the glass lid. Remove stirrer using a pot holder.

6. Immediately spoon jam into heated glass jars, leaving 1/4 in headspace. Cover with lids and rings.

7. Refrigerate up to 3 weeks, freeze up to 1 year, or fresh preserve and store up to 1 year.

# APRICOT JAM

*Apricots have a tart complex flavor that make this jam so versatile. You will find that it works so well in both savory and sweet applications.*

**PREP TIME:**
3 Minutes

**COOK TIME:**
21 Minutes

**MAKES:**
About 4 (8 oz) half pint jars.

**INGREDIENTS**

| | |
|---|---|
| 3 tbsp | classic powdered pectin |
| 2 2/3 cups | cored, peeled and finely chopped apricots |
| 1/2 tsp | butter |
| 3 1/3 cups | granulated sugar |

**DIRECTIONS**

1. Pre-measure all ingredients. Set aside.

2. Sprinkle pectin evenly in bottom of jam and jelly maker. Add chopped apricots evenly on top of pectin. Add butter to top.

3. Press JAM button on maker. The cook time will show 21 minutes. Press enter.

4. After 4 minutes, you will hear 4 short beeping sounds. Slowly add sugar to top of jam mixture while the stirrer is turning. Cover with glass lid.

**TIP:** Apricots have such a delicate skin, that if you like your jam to have more texture you can leave the skin on. Just make sure you chop the apricots finely.

5. After 17 more minutes, or until the jam maker beeps again, press cancel on the jam maker and unplug the maker. Carefully remove the glass lid. Remove stirrer using a pot holder.

6. Immediately spoon jam into heated glass jars, leaving 1/4 in headspace. Cover with lids and rings.

7. Refrigerate up to 3 weeks, freeze up to 1 year, or fresh preserve and store up to 1 year.

# Mixed berry Jam

*What is better than single berry jam, well it's a combination of three berries that bring all of your favorites into one delectable berry jam.*

**PREP TIME:**
2 Minutes

**COOK TIME:**
21 Minutes

**MAKES:**
About 4 (8 oz)
half pint jars.

**INGREDIENTS**

| | |
|---|---|
| 3 tbsp | classic powdered pectin |
| 1 cup | crushed blackberries (about 2 6-oz containers) |
| 1 cup | crushed raspberries (about 2 6-oz containers) |
| 2/3 cup | crushed strawberries (approximately 1 16-oz container) |
| 1/2 tsp | butter |
| 3 1/3 cups | granulated sugar |

**DIRECTIONS**

1. Pre-measure all ingredients. Set aside.

2. Sprinkle pectin evenly in bottom of jam and jelly maker. Add all crushed berries evenly on top of pectin. Add butter to top.

**TIP:** You can add more of your favorite berries to this recipe, but just make sure that the total measurement of all berries is 2 2/3 cups.

3. Press JAM button on maker. The cook time will show 21 minutes. Press enter.

4. After 4 minutes, you will hear 4 short beeping sounds. Slowly add sugar to top of berries while the stirrer is turning. Cover with glass lid.

5. After 17 more minutes, or until the jam maker beeps again, press cancel on the jam maker and unplug the maker. Carefully remove the glass lid. Remove stirrer using a pot holder.

6. Immediately spoon jam into heated glass jars, leaving 1/4 in headspace. Cover with lids and rings.

7. Refrigerate up to 3 weeks, freeze up to 1 year, or fresh preserve and store up to 1 year.

# 2
# LOWER SUGAR JAMS

# Low Sugar
# Blackberry Jam

*If you are trying to reduce the amount of sugar you eat, but still love your jams, you will love this blackberry jam that still delivers on taste.*

**PREP TIME:**
2 Minutes

**COOK TIME:**
21 Minutes

**MAKES:**
About 4 (8 oz) half pint jars

**INGREDIENTS**

| | |
|---|---|
| 3 tbsp | low or no sugar needed pectin |
| 3 2/3 cups | crushed blackberries (about five 6-oz containers) |
| 1/2 tsp | butter (optional) |
| 1 cup | granulated sugar |

**DIRECTIONS**

1. Pre-measure all ingredients. Set aside.

2. Sprinkle pectin evenly in bottom of jam and jelly maker. Add all crushed berries evenly on top of pectin. Add butter to top.

3. Press JAM button on maker. The cook time will show 21 minutes. Press enter.

**Tip:** You need to use low or no sugar pectin as stated in the recipe. Using regular pectin will cause your jam to not set properly.

4. After 4 minutes, you will hear 4 short beeping sounds. Slowly add sugar to top of berries while the stirrer is turning. Cover with glass lid.

5. After 17 more minutes, or until the jam maker beeps again, press cancel on the jam maker and unplug the maker. Carefully remove the glass lid. Remove stirrer using a pot holder.

6. Immediately spoon jam into heated glass jars, leaving 1/4 in headspace. Cover with lids and rings.

7. Refrigerate up to 3 weeks, freeze up to 1 year, or fresh preserve and store up to 1 year.

# LOW SUGAR
# MIXED BERRY JAM

*The marrying of flavors from the delightful mixture of berries gives the jam a wonderful sweet berry taste but with a lower amount of sugar.*

**PREP TIME:**
2 Minutes

**COOK TIME:**
21 Minutes

**MAKES:**
About 4 (8 oz)
half pint jars

### INGREDIENTS

| | |
|---|---|
| 3 tbsp | low or no sugar needed pectin |
| 1 1/2 cup | crushed blackberries (about 3 6-oz containers) |
| 1 1/2 cup | crushed raspberries (about 3 6-oz containers) |
| 2/3 cup | crushed strawberries (approximately 1 16-oz container) |
| 1/2 tsp | butter (optional) |
| 1 cup | granulated sugar |

### Directions

1. Pre-measure all ingredients. Set aside.

**Tip:** You can mix up the berry combinations to add more of your favorite, but just make sure that the total measurement of all berries combined is 3 2/3 cups.

2. Sprinkle pectin evenly in bottom of jam and jelly maker. Add all crushed berries evenly on top of pectin. Add butter to top.

3. Press JAM button on maker. The cook time will show 21 minutes. Press enter.

4. After 4 minutes, you will hear 4 short beeping sounds. Slowly add sugar to top of berries while the stirrer is turning. Cover with glass lid.

5. After 17 more minutes, or until the jam maker beeps again, press cancel on the jam maker and unplug the maker. Carefully remove the glass lid. Remove stirrer using a pot holder.

6. Immediately spoon jam into heated glass jars, leaving 1/4 in headspace. Cover with lids and rings.

7. Refrigerate up to 3 weeks, freeze up to 1 year, or fresh preserve and store up to 1 year.

# No Sugar
# Strawberry Jam

*A variation on a classic, this strawberry jam lets you enjoy and preserve fresh strawberries without adding sugar.*

**PREP TIME:**
1 Minute

**COOK TIME:**
21 Minutes

**MAKES:**
About 4 (8 oz) half pint jars

**INGREDIENTS**

| | |
|---|---|
| 3 tbsp | low or no-sugar needed pectin |
| 4 2/3 cups | crushed strawberries (about four 1-lb containers) |
| 1/2 tsp | butter (optional) |

**DIRECTIONS**

1. Pre-measure all ingredients. Set aside.

2. Sprinkle pectin evenly in bottom of jam and jelly maker. Add all crushed berries evenly on top of pectin. Add butter to top.

3. Press JAM button on maker. The cook time will show 21 minutes. Press enter.

4. After 4 minutes, you will hear 4 short beeping sounds. Cover with glass lid.

**Tips:** Choose strawberries that are dry, firm and fully ripe. Tops should be green and fresh looking.

Check the box to make sure there is no staining which could indicate overly ripe berries.

5. After 17 more minutes, or until the jam maker beeps again, press cancel on the jam maker and unplug the maker. Carefully remove the glass lid. Remove stirrer using a pot holder.

6. Immediately spoon jam into heated glass jars, leaving 1/4 in headspace. Cover with lids and rings.

7. Refrigerate up to 3 weeks, freeze up to 1 year, or fresh preserve and store up to 1 year.

# LOW SUGAR
# SPICED PEAR JAM

*A little cinnamon and nutmeg added to Barlett or Bosc pears in this jam celebrate the beginning of fall with this warm, deep flavored jam.*

**PREP TIME:**
2 Minutes

**COOK TIME:**
21 Minutes

**MAKES:**
About 4 (8 oz) half pint jars

### INGREDIENTS

| | |
|---|---|
| 1/2 tsp | ground cinnamon |
| 1/8 tsp | ground nutmeg |
| 1 cup | granulated sugar |
| 3 tbsp | low or no sugar needed pectin |
| 3 2/3 cups | crushed pears (about 7 medium pears) |
| 2 tbsp | bottled lemon juice |
| 1/2 tsp | butter (optional) |

### DIRECTIONS

1. Mix cinnamon and nutmeg into the cup of sugar. Set aside. Pre-measure all remaining ingredients and have them ready to go into the jam and jelly maker.

**Tip:**

Pears are best when ripened after picking. Pears should have a matte skin, not bright and shiny. Pears that are ripe and ready to use will have a slight give when you press near the neck with your thumb.

2. Sprinkle pectin evenly in bottom of jam and jelly maker. Add crushed pears evenly on top of pectin. Add butter to top.

3. Press JAM button on maker. The cook time will show 21 minutes. Press enter.

4. After 4 minutes, you will hear 4 short beeping sounds. Slowly add sugar mixture to top of pears while the stirrer is turning. Cover with glass lid.

5. After 17 more minutes, or until the jam maker beeps again, press cancel on the jam maker and unplug the maker. Carefully remove the glass lid. Remove stirrer using a pot holder.

6. Immediately spoon jam into heated glass jars, leaving 1/4 in headspace. Cover with lids and rings.

7. Refrigerate up to 3 weeks, freeze up to 1 year, or fresh preserve and store up to 1 year.

# Peach Cardamom Jam

*With less sugar and more peaches, you get a wonderful peachy taste in this jam. The cardamom adds very warm and pungent highlights.*

**PREP TIME:**
2 Minutes

**COOK TIME:**
21 Minutes

**MAKES:**
About 4 (8 oz) half pint jars

**INGREDIENTS**

| | |
|---|---|
| 1 cup | granulated sugar |
| 1 1/2 tsp | ground cardamom |
| 3 tsp | low or no-sugar needed pectin |
| 3 2/3 cup | chopped peaches |
| 2 tbsp | bottled lemon juice |
| 1/2 tsp | butter |
| 7/8 tsp | vanilla extract |

**DIRECTIONS**

1. Mix sugar lightly with ground cardamom. Set aside. Pre-measure all remaining ingredients and have them ready to go into the jam and jelly maker.

2. Sprinkle pectin evenly in bottom of jam and jelly maker. Add crushed peaches evenly on top of pectin. Add butter to top.

**Tip:**

Cardamom has a very complex, exotic taste. Measure carefully so you do not over power the flavor of the peaches. You can always adjust the amount for your taste buds.

3. Press JAM button on maker. The cook time will show 21 minutes. Press enter.

4. After 4 minutes, you will hear 4 short beeping sounds. Slowly add sugar mixture to top of pears while the stirrer is turning. Cover with glass lid.

5. After 17 more minutes, or until the jam maker beeps again, press cancel on the jam maker and unplug the maker. Carefully remove the glass lid. Remove stirrer using a pot holder.

6. Immediately spoon jam into heated glass jars, leaving 1/4 in headspace. Cover with lids and rings.

7. Refrigerate up to 3 weeks, freeze up to 1 year, or fresh preserve and store up to 1 year.

# Low Sugar Plum Jam

*With a panorama of colors and a diversity of taste, you will have endless variations you can explore in this plum jam.*

**PREP TIME:**
2 Minutes

**COOK TIME:**
21 Minutes

**MAKES:**
About 4 (8 oz) half pint jars

### INGREDIENTS

| | |
|---|---|
| 3 tbsp | low or no-sugar needed pectin |
| 3 2/3 cups | crushed plums (about 33 medium) |
| 1/2 tsp | butter (optional) |
| 1 cup | granulated sugar |

### DIRECTIONS

1. Pre-measure all ingredients. Set aside.

2. Sprinkle pectin evenly in bottom of jam and jelly maker. Add all crushed plums evenly on top of pectin. Add butter to top.

3. Press JAM button on maker. The cook time will show 21 minutes. Press enter.

**Tip:**

When choosing plums, look for ones that yield slightly to gentle pressure. They should have a rich color and may also have a slightly white bloom. Don't be concerned about the bloom, this indicates they haven't been overly handled.

4. After 4 minutes, you will hear 4 short beeping sounds. Slowly add sugar mixture to top of pears while the stirrer is turning. Cover with glass lid.

5. After 17 more minutes, or until the jam maker beeps again, press cancel on the jam maker and unplug the maker. Carefully remove the glass lid. Remove stirrer using a pot holder.

6. Immediately spoon jam into heated glass jars, leaving 1/4 in headspace. Cover with lids and rings.

7. Refrigerate up to 3 weeks, freeze up to 1 year, or fresh preserve and store up to 1 year.

# PEACH BLACKBERRY JAM

*Peaches and blackberries, with just a hint of cinnamon coalesce to make a richly colored, complex textured, tasty jam.*

**PREP TIME:**
2 Minutes

**COOK TIME:**
21 Minutes

**MAKES:**
About 4 (8 oz)
half pint jars

**INGREDIENTS**

| | |
|---|---|
| 2 cups | granulated sugar |
| 1 tsp | ground cinnamon |
| 3 tbsp | low or no-sugar needed pectin |
| 1 5/8 cups | crushed peaches (about 3 medium) |
| 1 5/8 cups | crushed blackberries (about two 6 oz containers) |
| 2 tbsp | bottled lemon juice |
| 1/2 tsp | butter (optional) |

**DIRECTIONS**

1. Mix sugar lightly with ground cinnamon. Set aside. Pre-measure all remaining ingredients and have them ready to go into the jam and jelly maker.

**Tip:**

To easily peel your peaches; bring a large pot of water to a boil. Prepare a large bowl with ice water. Using a slotted spoon, lower your peaches into the boiling water for 30 to 60 seconds. Remove your peaches using the slotted spoon and immediately put into the ice water. Let cool. Peach skin will easily pull off with your hand.

2. Sprinkle pectin evenly in bottom of jam and jelly maker. Add crushed peaches and blackberries evenly on top of pectin. Add butter to top

3. Press JAM button on maker. The cook time will show 21 minutes. Press enter.

4. After 4 minutes, you will hear 4 short beeping sounds. Slowly add sugar mixture to top of peach and berry mixture while the stirrer is turning. Cover with glass lid.

5. After 17 more minutes, or until the jam maker beeps again, press cancel on the jam maker and unplug the maker. Carefully remove the glass lid. Remove stirrer using a pot holder.

6. Immediately spoon jam into heated glass jars, leaving 1/4 in headspace. Cover with lids and rings.

7. Refrigerate up to 3 weeks, freeze up to 1 year, or fresh preserve and store up to 1 year.

# Rhubarb Peach Jam

*Slightly tart rhubarb and sweet peaches taste like they were meant to be together in this jam.*

**PREP TIME:**
3 Minutes

**COOK TIME:**
21 Minutes

**MAKES:**
About 4 (8 oz) half pint jars

## INGREDIENTS

| | |
|---|---|
| 3 tbsp | low or no-sugar needed pectin |
| 1 1/3 cups | diced rhubarb (about 2 to 3 stalks) |
| 2 1/3 cups | crushed peaches (about 3 medium) |
| 2 tbsp | bottled lemon juice |
| 1/2 tsp | butter (optional) |
| 1 cup | granulated sugar |

## DIRECTIONS

1. Pre-measure all ingredients. Set aside.

2. Sprinkle pectin evenly in bottom of jam and jelly maker. Add diced rhubarb and crushed peaches evenly on top of pectin. Add butter to top.

3. Press JAM button on maker. The cook time will show 21 minutes. Press enter.

**Tip:**

Use the deeper colored part of the rhubarb stalk.

If you want your rhubarb less coarse in the jam, cut it into thin slices and add to a food chopper until it is finely diced. Do not puree the rhubarb.

4. After 4 minutes, you will hear 4 short beeping sounds. Slowly add sugar mixture to top of rhubarb and peaches while the stirrer is turning. Cover with glass lid.

5. After 17 more minutes, or until the jam maker beeps again, press cancel on the jam maker and unplug the maker. Carefully remove the glass lid. Remove stirrer using a pot holder.

6. Immediately spoon jam into heated glass jars, leaving 1/4 in headspace. Cover with lids and rings.

7. Refrigerate up to 3 weeks, freeze up to 1 year, or fresh preserve and store up to 1 year.

# PINEAPPLE MANGO GREEN CHILI JAM

*Tropical fruits with a hint of heat impart a distinct and tantalizing taste. Serve this jam with a hearty cheese and sliced baguettes for a real treat.*

**PREP TIME:**
4 Minutes

**COOK TIME:**
21 Minutes

**MAKES:**
About 4 (8 oz) half pint jars

**INGREDIENTS**

| | |
|---|---|
| 3 tbsp | classic powdered pectin |
| 2 | 8 oz cans crushed pineapple, in pineapple juice |
| 1 1/4 cup | crushed mango (about 2 medium), peeled and cored |
| 1 | 4 oz can diced green chiles, roasted and peeled (mild, medium or hot) |
| 1/2 tsp | butter (optional) |
| 2 cups | granulated sugar |

**DIRECTIONS**

1. Pre-measure all ingredients. Set aside.

Use 2 cups crushed fresh pineapple (about 1 medium) instead of canned.

2. Sprinkle pectin evenly in bottom of jam and jelly maker. Add pineapple, mango and green chiles evenly on top of pectin. Add butter to top.

3. Press JAM button on maker. The cook time will show 21 minutes. Press enter.

4. After 4 minutes, you will hear 4 short beeping sounds. Slowly add sugar mixture to top fruit and chile mixture while the stirrer is turning. Cover with glass lid.

5. After 17 more minutes, or until the jam maker beeps again, press cancel on the jam maker and unplug the maker. Carefully remove the glass lid. Remove stirrer using a pot holder.

6. Immediately spoon jam into heated glass jars, leaving 1/4 in headspace. Cover with lids and rings.

7. Refrigerate up to 3 weeks, freeze up to 1 year, or fresh preserve and store up to 1 year.

# PEACH PEAR GINGER JAM

*Peaches and pears complement each other so well in this jam and impart a deep flavor and texture. Adding ginger adds a twist that will make you come back for more.*

**PREP TIME:**
3 Minutes

**COOK TIME:**
21 Minutes

**MAKES:**
About 4 (8 oz)
half pint jars

### INGREDIENTS

| | |
|---|---|
| 2 cups | granulated sugar |
| 2 tsp | grated fresh ginger |
| 3 tbsp | powdered fruit pectin |
| 2 cups | crushed peaches (about 2 medium) |
| 2/3 cup | crushed pears (about 2) |
| 2 tbsp | bottled lemon juice |
| 1/2 tsp | butter (optional) |

### DIRECTIONS

1. Mix sugar lightly with ground cinnamon. Set aside. Pre-measure all remaining ingredients and have them ready to go into the jam and jelly maker.

**Tip:**

To easily peel
your peaches
and pears;
bring a large
pot of water to
a boil. Prepare
a large bowl
with ice water.
Using a slotted
spoon, lower
fruit into the
boiling water
for 30 to 60
seconds.
Remove fruit
using the
slotted spoon
and put into
the ice water
immediately.
Let cool. Skins
will pull off
readily.

2. Sprinkle pectin evenly in bottom of jam and jelly maker. Add crushed peaches and pears evenly on top of pectin. Add butter to top.

3. Press JAM button on maker. The cook time will show 21 minutes. Press enter.

4. After 4 minutes, you will hear 4 short beeping sounds. Slowly add sugar mixture to top of fruit mixture while the stirrer is turning. Cover with glass lid.

5. After 17 more minutes, or until the jam maker beeps again, press cancel on the jam maker and unplug the maker. Carefully remove the glass lid. Remove stirrer using a pot holder.

6. Immediately spoon jam into heated glass jars, leaving 1/4 in headspace. Cover with lids and rings.

7. Refrigerate up to 3 weeks, freeze up to 1 year, or fresh preserve and store up to 1 year.

# 3
# SPECIALTY JAMS

# Pear Cranberry Orange Jam

*Make this brightly colored festive jam for holiday gift giving or to serve at your holiday celebrations.*

**PREP TIME:**
3 Minutes

**COOK TIME:**
21 Minutes

**MAKES:**
About 4 (8 oz) half pint jars

**INGREDIENTS**

| | |
|---|---|
| 3 tbsp | classic powdered pectin |
| 2 cups | crushed pears (about 2 lbs or six medium) |
| 2/3 cup | chopped fresh cranberries |
| 1/4 cup | orange juice |
| 1 tbsp | orange zest |
| 1/2 tsp | butter |
| 3 1/3 cups | granulated sugar |
| 1/2 tsp | cinnamon |

**DIRECTIONS**

1. Pre-measure all ingredients. Set aside.

**Tip:**

For a delightful gift, cover the top of the jar with festive cotton fabric and tie a thin ribbon around the neck of the jar. Make a card with the name of the jam and the year. Punch a hole in the card and slide in onto the ribbon.

2. Sprinkle pectin evenly in bottom of jam and jelly maker. Add crushed pears and chopped cranberries evenly on top of pectin. Pour in orange juice. Sprinkle with orange zest. Add butter to top of mixture.

3. Press JAM button on maker. The cook time will show 21 minutes. Press enter.

4. After 4 minutes, you will hear 4 short beeping sounds. Slowly add sugar to top of berries while the stirrer is turning. Sprinkle cinnamon over top of sugar. Cover with glass lid.

5. After 17 more minutes, or until the jam maker beeps again, press cancel on the jam maker and unplug the maker. Carefully remove the glass lid. Remove stirrer using a pot holder.

6. Immediately spoon jam into heated glass jars, leaving 1/4 in headspace. Cover with lids and rings.

7. Refrigerate up to 3 weeks, freeze up to 1 year, or fresh preserve and store up to 1 year.

# Zesty Blueberry Jam

*Delectable flavors are imparted in this jam with the pairing of blueberries and spices.*

**PREP TIME:**
2 Minutes

**COOK TIME:**
21 Minutes

**MAKES:**
About 4 (8 oz)
half pint jars

**INGREDIENTS**

| | |
|---|---|
| 1/8 tsp | ground star anise |
| 1/8 tsp | ground nutmeg |
| 3 cups | granulated sugar |
| 4 tbsp | classic powdered pectin |
| 2 2/3 cup | crushed blueberries (about 1 lb) |
| 2 tbsp | bottled lemon juice |
| 3 tbsp | cider vinegar (optional) |
| 1/2 tsp | butter (optional) |

**DIRECTIONS**

1. Mix the star anise and nutmeg lightly into the sugar. Set aside. Pre-measure all remaining ingredients and have them ready to go into the jam and jelly maker.

**TIP:**

You can substitute allspice for the star anise if you have that on hand.

2. Sprinkle pectin evenly in bottom of jam and jelly maker. Add crushed blueberries. Add lemon juice, vinegar and butter to top of mixture.

3. Press JAM button on maker. The cook time will show 21 minutes. Press enter.

4. After 4 minutes, you will hear 4 short beeping sounds. Slowly add sugar to top of jam mixture while the stirrer is turning. Cover with glass lid.

5. After 17 more minutes, or until the jam maker beeps again, press cancel on the jam maker and unplug the maker. Carefully remove the glass lid. Remove stirrer using a pot holder.

6. Immediately spoon jam into heated glass jars, leaving 1/4 in headspace. Cover with lids and rings.

7. Refrigerate up to 3 weeks, freeze up to 1 year, or fresh preserve and store up to 1 year.

# CINNAMON PEACH JAM

*Now you can enjoy the exquisite flavors of peach pie in a jam that you can indulge in for breakfast.*

**PREP TIME:**
2 Minutes

**COOK TIME:**
21 Minutes

**MAKES:**
About 4 (8 oz) half pint jars

### INGREDIENTS

| | |
|---|---|
| 3 tbsp | classic powdered pectin |
| 2 2/3 cups | finely chopped peaches |
| 2/3 tbsp | bottled lemon juice |
| 1/2 tsp | butter, optional |
| 1 2/3 cups | granulated sugar |
| 1/8 tsp | ground cinnamon |

### DIRECTIONS

1. Pre-measure all ingredients. Set aside.

2. Sprinkle pectin evenly in bottom of jam and jelly maker. Add finely chopped peaches. Add lemon juice. Top with butter.

3. Press JAM button on maker. The cook time will show 21 minutes. Press enter.

**Tip:**

To easily peel your peaches; Bring a large pot of water to a boil. Prepare a large bowl with ice water. Using a slotted spoon, lower your peaches into the boiling water for 30 to 60 seconds. Remove your peaches using the slotted spoon and immediately put into the ice water. Let cool. Peach skin will easily pull off with your hand.

4. After 4 minutes, you will hear 4 short beeping sounds. Slowly add sugar to top of jam mixture while the stirrer is turning. Add ground cinnamon. Cover with glass lid.

5. After 17 more minutes, or until the jam maker beeps again, press cancel on the jam maker and unplug the maker. Carefully remove the glass lid. Remove stirrer using a pot holder.

6. Immediately spoon jam into heated glass jars, leaving 1/4 in headspace. Cover with lids and rings.

7. Refrigerate up to 3 weeks, freeze up to 1 year, or fresh preserve and store up to 1 year.

# Strawberry Banana Jam

*Just a few ingredients shy of a yummy banana split. But you can always add this yummy jam to a scoop of ice cream for something close to the real-deal.*

**PREP TIME:**
2 Minutes

**COOK TIME:**
21 Minutes

**MAKES:**
About 4 (8 oz) half pint jars

**INGREDIENTS**

| | |
|---|---|
| 3 tbsp | classic powdered pectin |
| 1 1/3 cup | crushed strawberries (about 2 16-oz containers) |
| 1 1/3 cup | mashed bananas (about 2 fully ripe large bananas) |
| 3 tbsp | bottled lemon juice |
| 1/2 tsp | butter (optional) |
| 3 1/3 cups | granulated sugar |

**DIRECTIONS**

1. Pre-measure all ingredients. Set aside.

2. Sprinkle pectin evenly in bottom of jam and jelly maker. Add strawberries, bananas and lemon juice evenly on top of pectin. Add butter to top.

**Tip:**

Choose
bananas that
are fully
ripened but
aren't
completely
brown yet.
Many times
you can get a
deal on riper
bananas at
your local
grocer.

3. Press JAM button on maker. The cook time will show 21 minutes. Press enter.

4. After 4 minutes, you will hear 4 short beeping sounds. Slowly add sugar to top of jam mixture while the stirrer is turning. Cover with glass lid.

5. After 17 more minutes, or until the jam maker beeps again, press cancel on the jam maker and unplug the maker. Carefully remove the glass lid. Remove stirrer using a pot holder.

6. Immediately spoon jam into heated glass jars, leaving 1/4 in headspace. Cover with lids and rings.

7. Refrigerate up to 3 weeks, freeze up to 1 year, or fresh preserve and store up to 1 year.

# VERY BERRY CHERRY JAM

*A combination of berries that are sure to delight all of your senses are infused in this jam.*

**PREP TIME:**
3 Minutes

**COOK TIME:**
21 Minutes

**MAKES:**
About 4 (8 oz) half pint jars

**INGREDIENTS**

| | |
|---|---|
| 3 tbsp | classic powdered pectin |
| 1 1/3 cups | crushed sweet cherries (about 1 lb) |
| 2/3 cup | crushed strawberries (about one 1 lb container) |
| 2/3 cup | crushed raspberries (about one 6 oz container) |
| 2 tbsp | bottled lemon juice |
| 1/2 tsp | butter |
| 3 1/3 cups | granulated sugar |

**DIRECTIONS**

1. Pre-measure all ingredients. Set aside.

2. Sprinkle pectin evenly in bottom of jam and jelly maker. Add cherries, strawberries, raspberries and lemon juice evenly on top of pectin. Add butter to top.

**Tips:**

Instead of washing your raspberries, just roll them on a paper towel to get rid of any excess particles.

If you wash your berries, make sure they are completely dry before crushing and adding to the jam maker.

3. Press JAM button on maker. The cook time will show 21 minutes. Press enter.

4. After 4 minutes, you will hear 4 short beeping sounds. Slowly add sugar to top of jam mixture while the stirrer is turning. Cover with glass lid.

5. After 17 more minutes, or until the jam maker beeps again, press cancel on the jam maker and unplug the maker. Carefully remove the glass lid. Remove stirrer using a pot holder.

6. Immediately spoon jam into heated glass jars, leaving 1/4 in headspace. Cover with lids and rings.

7. Refrigerate up to 3 weeks, freeze up to 1 year, or fresh preserve and store up to 1 year.

# PEACH MELBA JAM

*The delectable combination of peaches and raspberries in this jam are reminiscent of a favorite dessert – the Peach Melba.*

**PREP TIME:**
4 Minutes

**COOK TIME:**
21 Minutes

**MAKES:**
About 4 (8 oz)
half pint jars

**INGREDIENTS**

| | |
|---|---|
| 3 tbsp | classic powdered pectin |
| 1 2/3 cups | pitted, peeled and finely chopped peaches (about 2 medium peaches |
| 1 cup | crushed raspberries (about 2 6 oz containers) |
| 1 tbsp | lemon juice, from bottle |
| 1/2 tsp | butter |
| 2 cups | granulated sugar |

**DIRECTIONS**

1. Pre-measure all ingredients. Set aside.

2. Sprinkle pectin evenly in bottom of jam and jelly maker. Add chopped peaches, crushed raspberries and lemon juice evenly on top of pectin. Add butter to top.

Serve this jam over ice cream for a true Peach Melba experience.

**Did you know:**

Peach Melba was created by famed French chef Auguste Escoffier who named it after his friend, Australian opera singer named Nellie Melba

3. Press JAM button on maker. The cook time will show 21 minutes. Press enter.

4. After 4 minutes, you will hear 4 short beeping sounds. Slowly add sugar to top of jam mixture while the stirrer is turning. Cover with glass lid.

5. After 17 more minutes, or until the jam maker beeps again, press cancel on the jam maker and unplug the maker. Carefully remove the glass lid. Remove stirrer using a pot holder.

6. Immediately spoon jam into heated glass jars, leaving 1/4 in headspace. Cover with lids and rings.

7. Refrigerate up to 3 weeks, freeze up to 1 year, or fresh preserve and store up to 1 year.

# GOOSEBERRY CARDAMOM JAM

*The tartness of gooseberry paired with the exotic, complex taste of cardamom give this jam a captivating flavor.*

**PREP TIME:**
2 Minutes

**COOK TIME:**
21 Minutes

**MAKES:**
About 4 (8 oz) half pint jars

**INGREDIENTS**

| | |
|---|---|
| 3 tbsp | classic powdered pectin |
| 2 2/3 cups | crushed gooseberries |
| 1/2 tsp | ground cardamom |
| 1 tsp | vanilla extract |
| 2 tbsp | bottled lime juice |
| 1/2 tsp | butter |
| 3 cups | granulated sugar |

**DIRECTIONS**

1. Pre-measure all ingredients. Set aside.

2. Sprinkle pectin evenly in bottom of jam and jelly maker. Add chopped crushed gooseberries, cardamom, vanilla extract and lime juice evenly on top of pectin. Add butter to top.

**Tip:**

Gooseberries have a range of flavors from mild to sweet. Choose gooseberries that have a more restrained flavor for this recipe as those will pair better with the other flavorings.

3. Press JAM button on maker. The cook time will show 21 minutes. Press enter.

4. After 4 minutes, you will hear 4 short beeping sounds. Slowly add sugar to top of jam mixture while the stirrer is turning. Cover with glass lid.

5. After 17 more minutes, or until the jam maker beeps again, press cancel on the jam maker and unplug the maker. Carefully remove the glass lid. Remove stirrer using a pot holder.

6. Immediately spoon jam into heated glass jars, leaving 1/4 in headspace. Cover with lids and rings.

7. Refrigerate up to 3 weeks, freeze up to 1 year, or fresh preserve and store up to 1 year.

# CARROT CAKE JAM

*What is better than carrot cake - Carrot cake jam that you can enjoy any time you would like.*

**PREP TIME:**
4 Minutes

**COOK TIME:**
21 Minutes

**MAKES:**
About 4 (8 oz)
half pint jars

**INGREDIENTS**

| | |
|---|---|
| 1 tsp | ground cinnamon |
| 1/2 tsp | ground nutmeg |
| 1/4 tsp | ground cloves |
| 3 cups | granulated sugar |
| 4 tbsp | classic powdered pectin |
| 1 1/2 cups | finely grated carrots |
| 1 1/2 cups | chopped pears |
| 1 3/4 cups | chopped pineapple, including juice |
| 3 tbsp | lemon juice, bottled |
| 1/2 tsp | butter |

**DIRECTIONS**
1. Mix the cinnamon, nutmeg and cloves lightly into the sugar. Set aside. Measure all remaining ingredients and have them ready to go into the jam maker.

**Tip:**

Spread cream
cheese over a
bagel, toasted
bread slice, or
English muffin
and then top
with this jam.
You will
almost think
you are eating
carrot cake.

2. Sprinkle pectin evenly in bottom of jam
   and jelly maker. Add grated carrots,
   chopped pears, chopped pineapple and
   lemon juice. Top with butter, if using.

3. Press JAM button on maker. The cook
   time will show 21 minutes. Press enter.

4. After 4 minutes, you will hear 4 short
   beeping sounds. Slowly add sugar to top
   of jam mixture while the stirrer is turning.
   Cover with glass lid.

5. After 17 more minutes, or until the jam
   maker beeps again, press cancel on the
   jam maker and unplug the maker.
   Carefully remove the glass lid. Remove
   stirrer using a pot holder.

6. Immediately spoon jam into heated glass
   jars, leaving 1/4 in headspace. Cover with
   lids and rings.

7. Refrigerate up to 3 weeks, freeze up to 1
   year, or fresh preserve and store up to 1
   year.

# TUTTI FRUTTI JAM

*The flavor and color or this jam remind me of some of my favorite childhood treats. Kids and adults alike are sure to enjoy this colorful jam.*

**PREP TIME:**
2 Minutes

**COOK TIME:**
21 Minutes

**MAKES:**
About 4 (8 oz) half pint jars

**INGREDIENTS**

| | |
|---|---|
| 3 tbsp | classic powdered pectin |
| 2 cups | chopped pears (about 4 medium) |
| 1 | large orange, peeled, seeds removed and pulp chopped |
| 1/2 cup | crushed, drained pineapple |
| 2 1/2 tbsp | chopped red maraschino cherries |
| 2 tbsp | bottled lemon juice |
| 1/2 tsp | butter |
| 3 cups | granulated sugar |

**DIRECTIONS**
1. Pre-measure all ingredients. Set aside.

For an even more colorful jam, use a combination of red and green maraschino cherries.

This jam is a treat served over ice cream. You can even add a dollop of whip cream and top with a maraschino cherry.

2. Sprinkle pectin evenly in bottom of jam and jelly maker. Add pears, oranges, pineapple, cherries and lemon juice. Top with butter if using.

3. Press JAM button on maker. The cook time will show 21 minutes. Press enter.

4. After 4 minutes, you will hear 4 short beeping sounds. Slowly add sugar to top of jam mixture while the stirrer is turning. Cover with glass lid.

5. After 17 more minutes, or until the jam maker beeps again, press cancel on the jam maker and unplug the maker. Carefully remove the glass lid. Remove stirrer using a pot holder.

6. Immediately spoon jam into heated glass jars, leaving 1/4 in headspace. Cover with lids and rings.

7. Refrigerate up to 3 weeks, freeze up to 1 year, or fresh preserve and store up to 1 year.

# Savory Scapes Jam

*This flavorful garlic-onion jam is fantastic on a cream cheese and bagel, in sandwiches or as a glaze on roasting chicken or pork dishes.*

**PREP TIME:**
2 Minutes

**COOK TIME:**
21 Minutes

**MAKES:**
About 4 (8 oz) half pint jars

**INGREDIENTS**

| | |
|---|---|
| 1 tbsp | freshly ground black pepper |
| 3/4 tsp | dried oregano leaves |
| 3/4 tsp | dried basil leaves |
| 3 cups | packed brown sugar |
| 4 tbsp | regular powdered fruit pectin |
| 4 cups | finely chopped scapes |
| 2/3 cup | dry white wine |
| 1/2 tsp | butter (optional) |
| 2/3 cup | balsamic vinegar |

**DIRECTIONS**

1. Mix the black pepper, oregano and basil lightly into the brown sugar. Set aside. Measure all remaining ingredients and have them ready to go into the jam maker.

**Tips:**

Baste a pork tenderloin with your scapes jam for a deep, rich flavor.

Use this jam in anything where you would have used a horseradish sauce or an onion glaze.

2. Sprinkle pectin evenly in bottom of jam maker. Add finely chopped scapes, dry white wine, and butter, if using.

3. Press JAM button on maker. The cook time will show 21 minutes. Press enter.

4. After 4 minutes, you will hear 4 short beeping sounds. Add balsamic vinegar. Slowly add brown sugar and spice mixture to the top of the scapes while the stirrer is turning. Cover with glass lid.

5. After 17 more minutes, or until the jam maker beeps again, press cancel on the jam maker and unplug the maker. Carefully remove the glass lid. Remove stirrer using a pot holder.

6. Immediately spoon jam into heated glass jars, leaving 1/4 in headspace. Cover with lids and rings.

7. Refrigerate up to 3 weeks, freeze up to 1 year, or fresh preserve and store up to 1 year.

Jams & Jellies: Preserving By The Pint In Minutes

# SECTION 2
# JELLIES

# CHAPTER 4
# FRUIT JELLIES

# GRAPE JELLY

*Get ready for the classic partner to peanut butter for a peanut butter and jelly sandwich. With your homemade jelly you will know exactly what is in it.*

**PREP TIME:**
1 Minutes

**COOK TIME:**
25 Minutes

**MAKES:**
About 4 (8 oz)
half pint jars

**INGREDIENTS**

| | |
|---|---|
| 3 cups | unsweetened grape juice, store bought |
| 4 tbsp | classic powdered pectin |
| 1/2 tsp | butter (optional) |
| 3 cups | granulated sugar |

**DIRECTIONS**

1. Pre-measure sugar. Set aside. Measure grape juice into quart size or larger glass measuring bowl. Whisk in pectin until blended but not dissolved.

2. Add juice to the jam and jelly maker. Add butter, if using, to reduce foaming. Do not cover.

3. Press JELLY button on maker. The cook time will show 25 minutes. Press enter.

**Tip:**

If you like a less sweet jelly or want to limit your sugar intake, use 1 1/2 cups sugar instead of the 3 cups. No other ingredients need to be adjusted. Your jelly will be less sweet and with a more intense grape flavor.

4. After 4 minutes, you will hear 4 short beeping sounds. Slowly add sugar to top of jelly mixture while the stirrer is turning. Cover with glass lid.

5. After 21 more minutes, or until the jam maker beeps again, press cancel on the jam maker and unplug the maker. Carefully remove the glass lid. Remove stirrer using a pot holder.

6. Skim foam from top of jelly, if necessary. Immediately spoon jelly into heated glass jelly jars, leaving 1/4 in headspace.

7. Refrigerate up to 3 weeks, freeze up to 1 year, or fresh preserve and store up to 1 year.

# BLACK CHERRY JELLY

*With a deep rich color and flavor, this cherry jelly is sure to please both the eyes and the palate.*

**PREP TIME:**
1 Minutes

**COOK TIME:**
25 Minutes

**MAKES:**
About 4 (8 oz)
half pint jars

## INGREDIENTS

| | |
|---|---|
| 3 cups | pure cherry juice, bottled and unsweetened |
| 4 tbsp | classic powdered pectin |
| 1/2 tsp | butter (optional) |
| 3 1/3 cups | granulated sugar |
| 2 tbsp | bottled lemon juice |

## DIRECTIONS

1. Pre-measure sugar. Set aside. Measure cherry juice into quart size or larger glass measuring bowl. Whisk in pectin until blended but not dissolved.

2. Add juice to the jam and jelly maker. Add butter, if using, to reduce foaming. Do not cover.

3. Press JELLY button on maker. The cook time will show 25 minutes. Press enter.

**Tip:**

Black cherry
jelly is a nice
accompaniment
to turkey and
pork dishes.
Try using black
cherry jelly
instead of
cranberry jelly
for your
holiday feasts.

4. After 4 minutes, you will hear 4 short beeping sounds. Slowly add sugar to top of jelly mixture while the stirrer is turning. Cover with glass lid.

5. After 21 more minutes, or until the jam maker beeps again, press cancel on the jam maker and unplug the maker. Carefully remove the glass lid. Remove stirrer using a pot holder.

6. Skim foam from top of jelly, if necessary. Immediately spoon jelly into heated glass jelly jars, leaving 1/4 in headspace.

7. Refrigerate up to 3 weeks, freeze up to 1 year, or fresh preserve and store up to 1 year.

# POMEGRANATE JELLY

*Pomegranates have been cherished for centuries for their exquisite taste, color and health benefits. With this quick and easy jam, you can enjoy them as often as you'd like.*

**PREP TIME:**
1 Minutes

**COOK TIME:**
25 Minutes

**MAKES:**
About 4 (8 oz) half pint jars

**INGREDIENTS**

| | |
|---|---|
| 3 cups | unsweetened pure pomegranate juice, store bought |
| 4 tsp | classic powdered pectin |
| 1/2 tbsp | butter (optional) |
| 3 1/3 cups | granulated sugar |

**DIRECTIONS**

1. Pre-measure sugar. Set aside. Measure pomegranate juice into quart size or larger glass measuring bowl. Whisk in pectin until blended but not dissolved.

2. Add juice to the jam and jelly maker. Add butter, if using, to reduce foaming. Do not cover.

3. Press JELLY button on maker. The cook time will show 25 minutes. Press enter.

**Variation:**

For a more tantalizing twist to this jelly, add 2 tsp orange liquor at the time you are adding the sugar. Pour liquor near the center of the mixture.

4. After 4 minutes, you will hear 4 short beeping sounds. Slowly add sugar to top of jelly mixture while the stirrer is turning. Cover with glass lid.

5. After 21 more minutes, or until the jam maker beeps again, press cancel on the jam maker and unplug the maker. Carefully remove the glass lid. Remove stirrer using a pot holder.

6. Skim foam from top of jelly, if necessary. Immediately spoon jelly into heated glass jelly jars, leaving 1/4 in headspace.

7. Refrigerate up to 3 weeks, freeze up to 1 year, or fresh preserve and store up to 1 year.

# APPLE JELLY

*What better way to keep the doctor away than a delightful serving of apple jelly daily.*

**PREP TIME:**
1 Minutes

**COOK TIME:**
25 Minutes

**MAKES:**
About 4 (8 oz)
half pint jars

**INGREDIENTS**

| | |
|---|---|
| 3 cups | unsweetened apple juice, store bought |
| 4 tbsp | classic powdered pectin |
| 1/2 tsp | butter (optional) |
| 3 1/3 cups | granulated sugar |

**DIRECTIONS**

1. Pre-measure sugar. Set aside. Measure apple juice into quart size or larger glass measuring bowl. Whisk in pectin until blended but not dissolved.

2. Add juice to the jam and jelly maker. Add butter, if using, to reduce foaming. Do not cover.

3. Press JELLY button on maker. The cook time will show 25 minutes. Press enter.

**Tips:**

Room temperature juice works best for making jelly. You can use concentrated or regular juice, but it should be unsweetened and 100% juice.

4. After 4 minutes, you will hear 4 short beeping sounds. Slowly add sugar to top of jelly mixture while the stirrer is turning. Cover with glass lid.

5. After 21 more minutes, or until the jam maker beeps again, press cancel on the jam maker and unplug the maker. Carefully remove the glass lid. Remove stirrer using a pot holder.

6. Skim foam from top of jelly, if necessary. Immediately spoon jelly into heated glass jelly jars, leaving 1/4 in headspace.

7. Refrigerate up to 3 weeks, freeze up to 1 year, or fresh preserve and store up to 1 year.

# REDUCED SUGAR PLUM JELLY

*Why wait for sugar plum fairies to come dancing through your head when you can enjoy this magical jelly any time you like.*

**PREP TIME:**
1 Minutes

**COOK TIME:**
25 Minutes

**MAKES:**
About 4 (8 oz)
half pint jars

**INGREDIENTS**

| | |
|---|---|
| 3 cups | unsweetened plum juice, store bought |
| 4 tbsp | classic powdered pectin |
| 1/2 tsp | butter (optional) |
| 2 cups | granulated sugar |

**DIRECTIONS**

1. Pre-measure sugar. Set aside. Measure plum juice into quart size or larger glass measuring bowl. Whisk in pectin until blended but not dissolved.

2. Add juice to the jam and jelly maker. Add butter, if using, to reduce foaming. Do not cover.

3. Press JELLY button on maker. The cook time will show 25 minutes. Press enter.

**Tip:**

If you like a little bit sweeter jelly you can use up to 3 1/3 cups of sugar. Try it in smaller amounts to see what flavor you like best. Add more sugar instead of buying sweetened juice to get your added sweetness.

4. After 4 minutes, you will hear 4 short beeping sounds. Slowly add sugar to top of jelly mixture while the stirrer is turning. Cover with glass lid.

5. After 21 more minutes, or until the jam maker beeps again, press cancel on the jam maker and unplug the maker. Carefully remove the glass lid. Remove stirrer using a pot holder.

6. Skim foam from top of jelly, if necessary. Immediately spoon jelly into heated glass jelly jars, leaving 1/4 in headspace.

7. Refrigerate up to 3 weeks, freeze up to 1 year, or fresh preserve and store up to 1 year.

# BOYSENBERRY JELLY

*Enjoy this rich and deeply flavored jam that has hints of raspberries and blackberries and a deep tantalizing color.*

**PREP TIME:**
1 Minutes

**COOK TIME:**
25 Minutes

**MAKES:**
About 4 (8 oz) half pint jars

**INGREDIENTS**

| | |
|---|---|
| 3 cups | unsweetened pure boysenberry juice, store bought |
| 4 tsp | classic powdered pectin |
| 1/2 tbsp | butter (optional) |
| 3 1/3 cups | granulated sugar |

**DIRECTIONS**

1. Pre-measure sugar. Set aside. Measure boysenberry juice into quart size or larger glass measuring bowl. Whisk in pectin until blended but not dissolved.

2. Add juice to the jam and jelly maker. Add butter, if using, to reduce foaming. Do not cover.

3. Press JELLY button on maker. The cook time will show 25 minutes. Press enter.

**Tip:**

Serve this jam
in mini tart
cups or phyllo
cups for a
sweet and
beautiful
dessert. Top
with a berry
and a fresh
mint leaf for
decoration.

4. After 4 minutes, you will hear 4 short
   beeping sounds. Slowly add sugar to top
   of jelly mixture while the stirrer is
   turning. Cover with glass lid.

5. After 21 more minutes, or until the jam
   maker beeps again, press cancel on the
   jam maker and unplug the maker.
   Carefully remove the glass lid. Remove
   stirrer using a pot holder.

6. Skim foam from top of jelly, if necessary.
   Immediately spoon jelly into heated glass
   jelly jars, leaving 1/4 in headspace.

7. Refrigerate up to 3 weeks, freeze up to 1
   year, or fresh preserve and store up to 1
   year.

# CHAPTER 5
# SAVORY JELLIES

# FESTIVE PEPPER JELLY

*Sprinkles of red and green peppers make this a very colorful and fiery tasting jelly.*

**PREP TIME:**
1 Minutes

**COOK TIME:**
25 Minutes

**MAKES:**
About 4 (8 oz)
half pint jars

**INGREDIENTS**

| | |
|---|---|
| 3 tbsp | classic powdered pectin |
| 1 1/3 cups | finely chopped red bell peppers (about 2 peppers) |
| 3/4 cup | finely chopped green bell peppers (about 1 pepper) |
| 1 | 4 oz can green chile peppers |
| 2/3 cup | white wine vinegar |
| 1/2 tsp | butter |
| 2 cups | granulated sugar |

**DIRECTIONS**

1. Pre-measure all ingredients. Set aside.

2. Sprinkle pectin evenly in bottom of jam and jelly maker. Add chopped red, green and chile peppers. Add white wine vinegar to top of peppers. Add butter on top of mixture.

Spread this jam over blocks of cream cheese and serve with crackers for a festive appetizer.

The color and texture of this jelly is prized for gift giving and receiving. Attach a label and ribbon and you have special gift.

3. Press JELLY button on maker. The cook time will show 25 minutes. Press enter.

4. After 4 minutes, you will hear 4 short beeping sounds. Slowly add sugar to top of jelly mixture while the stirrer is turning. Cover with glass lid.

5. After 21 more minutes, or until the jam maker beeps again, press cancel on the jam maker and unplug the maker. Carefully remove the glass lid. Remove stirrer using a pot holder.

6. Skim foam from top of jelly, if necessary. Immediately spoon jelly into heated glass jelly jars, leaving 1/4 in headspace.

7. Refrigerate up to 3 weeks, freeze up to 1 year, or fresh preserve and store up to 1 year.

# JALAPENO LIME JELLY

*If you like it hot, this jelly will certainly satisfy your taste buds. The lime juice adds a nice citrusy twist.*

**PREP TIME:**
3 Minutes

**COOK TIME:**
25 Minutes

**MAKES:**
About 4 (8 oz)
half pint jars

**INGREDIENTS**

| | |
|---|---|
| 5 tbsp | classic powdered pectin |
| 1 1/4 cups | minced jalapeno peppers, cored and seeded (about 12 jalapenos) |
| 1 1/2 cups | cider vinegar |
| 1/4 cup | bottled lime juice |
| 1/2 tsp | butter |
| 3 1/2 cups | granulated sugar |

**DIRECTIONS**

1. Pre-measure all ingredients. Set aside.

2. Sprinkle pectin evenly in bottom of jam and jelly maker. Add jalapeno peppers to top of pectin. Add vinegar and lime juice to top of peppers. Add butter on top of mixture.

**Tip:**

Always use rubber gloves when handling hot peppers so you do not burn your skin. Take care that you do not touch anything else with your rubber gloves.

3. Press JELLY button on maker. The cook time will show 25 minutes. Press enter.

4. After 4 minutes, you will hear 4 short beeping sounds. Slowly add sugar to top of jelly mixture while the stirrer is turning. Cover with glass lid.

5. After 21 more minutes, or until the jam maker beeps again, press cancel on the jam maker and unplug the maker. Carefully remove the glass lid. Remove stirrer using a pot holder.

6. Skim foam from top of jelly, if necessary. Immediately spoon jelly into heated glass jelly jars, leaving 1/4 in headspace.

7. Refrigerate up to 3 weeks, freeze up to 1 year, or fresh preserve and store up to 1 year.

# HORSERADISH JELLY

*This easy to make jelly is the perfect accompaniment to roast beef or ham sandwiches.*

**PREP TIME:**
1 Minutes

**COOK TIME:**
25 Minutes

**MAKES:**
About 4 (8 oz) half pint jars

**INGREDIENTS**

| | |
|---|---|
| 1 2/3 cups | no sugar added apple juice, store bought |
| 1 1/4 cup | water |
| 4 tbsp | low or no-sugar needed pectin |
| 1 1/4 cups | granulated sugar |
| 1/2 tsp | butter (optional) |
| 1/4 cup + 1 tbsp | apple cider vinegar |
| 1/3 cup | prepared horseradish |

**DIRECTIONS**

1. Measure apple juice and water into quart size or larger glass measuring bowl. Whisk in pectin until blended but not dissolved. Pre-measure all remaining ingredients. Set aside.

**Tip:**

Make sure to use prepared horseradish not a horseradish sauce or other variation that has added ingredients. If you can find horseradish in the refrigerated section of your grocery store, that version will most like have the least added ingredients and preservatives.

2. Add juice to the jam and jelly maker. Add butter, if using, to reduce foaming. Do not cover.

3. Press JELLY button on maker. The cook time will show 25 minutes. Press enter.

4. After 4 minutes, you will hear 4 short beeping sounds. Slowly add sugar to top of jelly mixture while the stirrer is turning. Cover with glass lid.

5. After 17 minutes, or until the jam and jelly maker shows 4 minutes remaining, add apple cider vinegar and horseradish to jelly mixture.

6. Skim foam from top of jelly, if necessary. Immediately spoon jelly into heated glass jelly jars, leaving 1/4 in headspace.

7. Refrigerate up to 3 weeks, freeze up to 1 year, or fresh preserve and store up to 1 year.

# MINT JELLY

*Classic and a staple for lamb lovers everywhere, this mint jelly adds just the right amount of fresh mint for a delectable accompaniment to your entrees.*

**PREP TIME:**
2 Minutes

**INACTIVE TIME:**
2 hours 20 minutes

**COOK TIME:**
25 Minutes

**MAKES:**
About 4 (8 oz) half pint jars

### INGREDIENTS

| | |
|---|---|
| 1 1/2 cups | finely chopped, packed mint |
| 3 1/4 cups | water |
| 4 tbsp | classic powdered pectin |
| 1/2 tsp | butter (optional) |
| 4 cups | granulated sugar |

### DIRECTIONS

1. Pre-measure sugar. Set aside. In a medium-size kettle, add mint and water. Bring to a boil. Remove from heat and cover. Let stand 20 minutes to steep.

2. Line a sieve or strainer with cheesecloth or a dampened jelly bag. Place over a large bowl. Pour mint mixture into prepared strainer. Let drip into bowl, undisturbed, for 2 hours, or until you have 3 cups of liquid. Do not squeeze mixture or your jelly may become cloudy.

**Tip:**

If you prefer a stronger green coloring in this jam, you can add 1/4 tsp green food coloring. For a natural green coloring additive, use a liquid chlorophyll.

3. Add pectin, mint liquid and butter to jam and jelly maker

4. Press JELLY button on maker. The cook time will show 25 minutes. Press enter.

5. After 4 minutes, you will hear 4 short beeping sounds. Slowly add sugar to top of jelly mixture while the stirrer is turning. Cover with glass lid.

6. After 21 more minutes, or until the jam maker beeps again, press cancel on the jam maker and unplug the maker. Carefully remove the glass lid. Remove stirrer using a pot holder.

7. Skim foam from top of jelly, if necessary. Immediately spoon jelly into heated glass jelly jars, leaving 1/4 in headspace.

8. Refrigerate up to 3 weeks, freeze up to 1 year, or fresh preserve and store up to 1 year.

# CANDY APPLE JELLY

*Sugar and spice and everything nice make this rosy colored jelly great for gift giving.*

**PREP TIME:**
1 Minutes

**COOK TIME:**
25 Minutes

**MAKES:**
About 4 (8 oz)
half pint jars

**INGREDIENTS**

| | |
|---|---|
| 4 tbsp | powdered fruit pectin |
| 2 3/4 cups | unsweetened apple juice |
| 1/3 cup | red hot candies |
| 1/2 tsp | butter |
| 3 1/3 cups | granulated sugar |

**DIRECTIONS**

1. Pre-measure sugar and candies. Set aside. Measure apple juice into quart size or larger glass measuring bowl. Whisk in pectin until blended but not dissolved.

2. Add juice and red hot candies to the jam and jelly maker. Do not cover.

3. Press JELLY button on maker. The cook time will show 25 minutes. Press enter.

**Tip:**

For creative gift giving, add a decorative label and tie a ribbon around the neck of the jar.

4. After 4 minutes, you will hear 4 short beeping sounds. Slowly add sugar to top of jelly mixture while the stirrer is turning. Cover with glass lid.

5. After 21 more minutes, or until the jam maker beeps again, press cancel on the jam maker and unplug the maker. Carefully remove the glass lid. Remove stirrer using a pot holder.

6. Skim foam from top of jelly and any remaining red hot candy remnants, if necessary. Immediately spoon jelly into heated glass jelly jars, leaving 1/4 in headspace.

7. Refrigerate up to 3 weeks, freeze up to 1 year, or fresh preserve and store up to 1 year.

# WRANGLER JELLY

*Get ready for a rockin' rodeo good time with the sweetness of pineapple paired with a kick of heat.*

| | |
|---|---|
| **PREP TIME:** 2 Minutes | |
| **COOK TIME:** 25 Minutes | |
| **MAKES:** About 4 (8 oz) half pint jars | |

**INGREDIENTS**

| | |
|---|---|
| 3 tbsp | regular powdered fruit pectin |
| 1 | 20 oz can of crushed pineapple |
| 3 | ground jalapenos, 2 jalapenos with seeds removed, 1 jalapeno with seeds intact |
| 1/2 tsp | ground cayenne pepper |
| 1/2 tsp | butter |
| 3 1/3 cups | granulated sugar |

**DIRECTIONS**

1. Pre-measure all ingredients. Set aside.

2. Sprinkle pectin evenly in bottom of jam and jelly maker. Add pineapple, jalapenos and cayenne pepper to top of pectin. Add butter on top of mixture.

Use this jelly on cheese and crackers, as a glaze on ham, or as a glaze or dip for chicken wings. You can also add it to cream cheese as a nice appetizer dip. Many types of sandwiches, including a breakfast sandwich with ham and egg on an English muffin.

3. Press JELLY button on maker. The cook time will show 25 minutes. Press enter.

4. After 4 minutes, you will hear 4 short beeping sounds. Slowly add sugar to top of jelly mixture while the stirrer is turning. Cover with glass lid.

5. After 21 more minutes, or until the jam maker beeps again, press cancel on the jam maker and unplug the maker. Carefully remove the glass lid. Remove stirrer using a pot holder.

6. Skim foam from top of jelly, if necessary. Immediately spoon jelly into heated glass jelly jars, leaving 1/4 in headspace.

7. Refrigerate up to 3 weeks, freeze up to 1 year, or fresh preserve and store up to 1 year.

# MULLED CIDER JELLY

*When the weather starts to get cooler there is nothing more inviting for your senses than the smell of simmering apple cider and spices.*

**PREP TIME:**
2 Minutes

**COOK TIME:**
25 Minutes

**MAKES:**
About 4 (8 oz) half pint jars

### INGREDIENTS

| | |
|---|---|
| 3 cups | apple cider |
| 4 tbsp | classic powdered pectin |
| 1/2 tsp | butter |
| 1 1/2 cups | granulated sugar |
| 3/4 tsp | ground cinnamon |
| 1/4 tsp | ground nutmeg |
| 1/4 tsp | ground allspice |
| 1/4 | ground cloves |

### DIRECTIONS

1. Measure apple cider into quart size or larger glass measuring bowl. Whisk in pectin until blended but not dissolved.

2. Add juice to the jam and jelly maker. Add butter, if using, to reduce foaming. Do not cover.

Don't be tempted to buy a mulling spice. Their spice combinations vary widely and may not give you the results you desire.

Coriander and cardamom also work well as a mulling spice. Just adjust all your spice measurements accordingly.

3. Press JELLY button on maker. The cook time will show 25 minutes. Press enter.

4. While jelly is stirring, measure sugar and spices. Gently stir spices into sugar.

5. After 4 minutes, you will hear 4 short beeping sounds. Slowly add sugar to top of jelly mixture while the stirrer is turning. Cover with glass lid.

6. After 21 more minutes, or until the jam maker beeps again, press cancel on the jam maker and unplug the maker. Carefully remove the glass lid. Remove stirrer using a pot holder.

7. Skim foam from top of jelly, if necessary. Immediately spoon jelly into heated glass jelly jars, leaving 1/4 in headspace.

8. Refrigerate up to 3 weeks, freeze up to 1 year, or fresh preserve and store up to 1 year.

# TOMATO SRIRACHA JELLY

*Tomatoes, spicy sriracha sauce and fresh basil coalesce into a jelly that will leave you warm inside and smiling on the outside.*

**PREP TIME:**
2 Minutes

**COOK TIME:**
25 Minutes

**MAKES:**
About 4 (8 oz) half pint jars

### INGREDIENTS

| | |
|---|---|
| 3 tbsp | regular powdered fruit pectin |
| 2 cups | tomato juice (about 3 lbs or 8 medium tomatoes to make juice) |
| 1/2 tsp | salt |
| 2 tbsp | lemon juice |
| 1 tsp | sriracha sauce |
| 1/2 tsp | butter (optional) |
| 3 cups | granulated sugar |
| 1/2 cup | coarsely chopped fresh basil |

### DIRECTIONS
1. Pre-measure all ingredients. Set aside.

Use this jelly on hamburgers and sandwiches or as a dipping sauce just like you would ketchup but with a little extra heat.

Use organic tomatoes or ones grown in your own garden for a healthier alternative.

2. Sprinkle pectin evenly in bottom of jam and jelly maker. In order, add tomato juice, salt, lemon juice and sriracha sauce to the top of the pectin. Add butter, if using to reduce foaming.

3. Press JELLY button on maker. The cook time will show 25 minutes. Press enter.

4. While jelly is stirring, measure sugar and basil. Gently stir basil into sugar.

5. After 4 minutes, you will hear 4 short beeping sounds. Slowly add sugar and basil mixture to top of jelly mixture while the stirrer is turning. Cover with glass lid.

6. After 21 more minutes, or until the jam maker beeps again, press cancel on the jam maker and unplug the maker. Carefully remove the glass lid. Remove stirrer using a pot holder.

7. Skim foam from top of jelly, if necessary. Immediately spoon jelly into heated glass jelly jars, leaving 1/4 in headspace.

8. Refrigerate up to 3 weeks, freeze up to 1 year, or fresh preserve and store up to 1 year.

# CHAPTER 6

# HAPPY HOUR PRESERVES

# TROPICAL DAIQUIRI JAM

*Strawberries, kiwi, pineapple and lime coalesce into a very tropical deep flavored jam.*

**PREP TIME:**
3 Minutes

**COOK TIME:**
21 Minutes

**MAKES:**
About 4 (8 oz) half pint jars

## INGREDIENTS

| | |
|---|---|
| 4 tbsp | classic powdered pectin |
| 1 cup | crushed strawberries (about one 1-lb container) |
| 1 cup | crushed kiwi (about 3 kiwi) |
| 1/3 cup | unsweetened pineapple juice |
| 1/4 cup | lime juice |
| 1 tsp | pure rum extract |
| 1/2 tsp | butter |
| 2 cups | granulated sugar |

## DIRECTIONS

1. Pre-measure all ingredients. Set aside.

2. Sprinkle pectin evenly in bottom of jam maker. Add strawberries, kiwi, lime juice and rum extract. Top with butter if using.

**Tips:**

You can substitute 3 tbsp rum for the rum extract.

Serve on top of ice cream for a summertime dessert.

3. Press JAM button on maker. The cook time will show 21 minutes. Press enter.

4. After 4 minutes, you will hear 4 short beeping sounds. Slowly add sugar to top of jam mixture while the stirrer is turning. Cover with glass lid.

5. After 17 more minutes, or until the jam maker beeps again, press cancel on the jam maker and unplug the maker. Carefully remove the glass lid. Remove stirrer using a pot holder.

6. Immediately spoon jam into heated glass jars, leaving 1/4 in headspace. Cover with lids and rings.

7. Refrigerate up to 3 weeks, freeze up to 1 year, or fresh preserve and store up to 1 year.

# PINA COLADA JAM

*If you are ready to reminisce about a fabulous island vacation while sipping drinks by the pool, then this is the jam for you to make.*

**PREP TIME:**
3 Minutes

**COOK TIME:**
21 Minutes

**MAKES:**
About 4 (8 oz)
half pint jars

**INGREDIENTS**

| | |
|---|---|
| 3 tbsp | classic powdered pectin |
| 4 | 8 oz cans crushed pineapple in 100% juice |
| 1/3 cup | coconut rum |
| 1/2 tsp | butter |
| 2 cups | granulated sugar |

**DIRECTIONS**

1. Pre-measure all ingredients. Set aside.

2. Sprinkle pectin evenly in bottom of jam maker. Add crushed pineapple and coconut water. Top with butter if using.

3. Press JAM button on maker. The cook time will show 21 minutes. Press enter.

**Variations:**

Use coconut water instead of rum.

Use 3 1/2 cups fresh crushed pineapple (about 1 medium) instead of canned.

If you want more texture and coconut, reduce the pineapple to 3 1/4 cups and add 1/4 cup coarsely chopped shredded coconut.

4. After 4 minutes, you will hear 4 short beeping sounds. Slowly add sugar to top of jam mixture while the stirrer is turning. Cover with glass lid.

5. After 17 more minutes, or until the jam maker beeps again, press cancel on the jam maker and unplug the maker. Carefully remove the glass lid. Remove stirrer using a pot holder.

6. Immediately spoon jam into heated glass jars, leaving 1/4 in headspace. Cover with lids and rings.

7. Refrigerate up to 3 weeks, freeze up to 1 year, or fresh preserve and store up to 1 year.

# Black Forest Jam

*A decadent jam just like its namesake dessert. Try this jam for a rich and luscious dessert-like taste.*

**Prep Time:**
3 Minutes

**Cook Time:**
21 Minutes

**Makes:**
About 4 (8 oz)
half pint jars

### Ingredients

| | |
|---|---|
| 2 cups | granulated sugar |
| 1/4 cup | unsweetened cocoa powder |
| 4 tbsp | regular classic fruit pectin |
| 3 1/4 cups | crushed sweet cherries (about 2 lbs) |
| 2 tbsp | bottled lemon juice |
| 2 tbsp | cherry brandy (or 1/2 tsp brandy extract |
| 1/2 tsp | butter (optional) |

### Directions

1. Mix together sugar and unsweetened cocoa powder. Set aside.

2. Sprinkle pectin evenly in bottom of jam and jelly maker. In order, add crushed cherries, lemon juice and brandy to top of pectin. Top with butter, if using to reduce foaming.

**Tips:**

Cover all surfaces before pitting your cherries or work in a very deep bowl or sink. Juicy cherries are wonderful, but very messy.

Cut the cherries with a kitchen shears or knife to make them easier and less messy to crush. Use a potato masher to crush them.

3. Press JAM button on maker. The cook time will show 21 minutes. Press enter.

4. After 4 minutes, you will hear 4 short beeping sounds. Slowly add sugar and cocoa mixture to top of jam mixture while the stirrer is turning. Cover with glass lid.

5. After 17 more minutes, or until the jam maker beeps again, press cancel on the jam maker and unplug the maker. Carefully remove the glass lid. Remove stirrer using a pot holder.

6. Immediately spoon jam into heated glass jars, leaving 1/4 in headspace. Cover with lids and rings.

7. Refrigerate up to 3 weeks, freeze up to 1 year, or fresh preserve and store up to 1 year.

# PEACH CINNAMON JAM

*Cinnamon adds just the right kiss of flavor to peaches to give this jam a deep, comforting and down-home flavor.*

**PREP TIME:**
3 Minutes

**COOK TIME:**
21 Minutes

**MAKES:**
About 4 (8 oz)
half pint jars

**INGREDIENTS**

| | |
|---|---|
| 3 tbsp | classic powdered fruit pectin |
| 3 1/4 | cups crushed peaches (about 2 lbs or six medium) |
| 2 tbsp | bottled lemon juice |
| 2 tbsp | cinnamon whiskey |
| 1/2 tsp | butter |
| 2 cups | granulated sugar |

**DIRECTIONS**

1. Pre-measure sugar. Set aside.

2. Sprinkle pectin evenly in bottom of jam and jelly maker. Add crushed peaches, lemon juice and cinnamon whiskey evenly on top of pectin. Top with butter, if using to reduce foaming..

3. Press JAM button on maker. The cook time will show 21 minutes. Press enter.

**Tips:**

Serve this jam on top of shortcake rounds and top with a dollop of sour cream for a delightful dessert.

To make it easier to crush your peaches, peel and pit peaches, then coarsely chop peaches, and then crush with a potato masher.

4. After 4 minutes, you will hear 4 short beeping sounds. Slowly add sugar to top of jam mixture while the stirrer is turning. Cover with glass lid.

5. After 17 more minutes, or until the jam maker beeps again, press cancel on the jam maker and unplug the maker. Carefully remove the glass lid. Remove stirrer using a pot holder.

6. Immediately spoon jam into heated glass jars, leaving 1/4 in headspace. Cover with lids and rings.

7. Refrigerate up to 3 weeks, freeze up to 1 year, or fresh preserve and store up to 1 year.

# SPIRITED SHIRLEY TEMPLE JELLY

*If you enjoyed the Shirley Temple drink as a kid, then this spirits added jelly version will bring back fond indulgent memories.*

**PREP TIME:**
1 Minutes

**COOK TIME:**
25 Minutes

**MAKES:**
About 4 (8 oz) half pint jars

### INGREDIENTS

| | |
|---|---|
| 3 cups | unsweetened pomegranate juice, store bought |
| 4 tbsp | classic powdered pectin |
| 1 tbsp | orange liquor |
| 1/2 tsp | ground ginger (optional) |
| 1/2 tsp | butter (optional) |
| 3 cups | granulated sugar |

### DIRECTIONS

1. Pre-measure sugar. Set aside.

2. Measure pomegranate juice into quart size or larger glass measuring bowl. Whisk in pectin until blended but not dissolved.

## Variation:

Add the ground ginger if you like your Shirley Temples made with ginger ale. If you prefer a lemon-lime soda flavor instead, add lime and lemon zest.

3. Add juice to the jam and jelly maker. Add orange liquor. Add ground ginger and butter, if using. Do not cover.

4. Press JELLY button on maker. The cook time will show 25 minutes. Press enter.

5. After 4 minutes, you will hear 4 short beeping sounds. Slowly add sugar to top of jelly mixture while the stirrer is turning. Cover with glass lid.

6. After 21 more minutes, or until the jam maker beeps again, press cancel on the jam maker and unplug the maker. Carefully remove the glass lid. Remove stirrer using a pot holder.

7. Skim foam from top of jelly, if necessary. Immediately spoon jelly into heated glass jelly jars, leaving 1/4 in headspace.

8. Refrigerate up to 3 weeks, freeze up to 1 year, or fresh preserve and store up to 1 year.

# Strawberry Sriracha Margarita Jam

*If you are a fan of Rooster sauce, you need to check out this jam made with a combination of heat and sweet to send your taste buds to Margaritaville.*

**Prep Time:**
3 Minutes

**Cook Time:**
21 Minutes

**Makes:**
About 4 (8 oz)
half pint jars

**Ingredients**

| | |
|---|---|
| 2 cups | granulated sugar |
| 3 tbsp | classic powdered pectin |
| 3 1/3 cups | crushed strawberries (about two 1 pound containers) |
| 1/4 cup | tequila |
| 2 tbsp | orange liquor |
| 2 tbsp | bottled lime juice |
| 1/2 tsp | sriracha sauce |
| 1/2 tsp | butter |

**Directions**
1. Pre-measure sugar. Set aside.

**Tip:**

Alcohol intensifies the heat of the sriracha sauce. So for those hardy Rooster lovers out there, on your first try do not be tempted to add more sriracha sauce unless you know you want a lot of heat.

2. Sprinkle pectin evenly in bottom of jam and jelly maker. In order, add crushed strawberries, orange liquor, lime juice and sriracha evenly on top of pectin. Top with butter, if using to reduce foaming..

3. Press JAM button on maker. The cook time will show 21 minutes. Press enter.

4. After 4 minutes, you will hear 4 short beeping sounds. Slowly add sugar to top of jam mixture while the stirrer is turning. Cover with glass lid.

5. After 17 more minutes, or until the jam maker beeps again, press cancel on the jam maker and unplug the maker. Carefully remove the glass lid. Remove stirrer using a pot holder.

6. Immediately spoon jam into heated glass jars, leaving 1/4 in headspace. Cover with lids and rings.

7. Refrigerate up to 3 weeks, freeze up to 1 year, or fresh preserve and store up to 1 year.

To get more information and order your Ball® FreshTECH Automatic Jam and Jelly Maker visit www.amzn.to/1p729He or with your smartphone, scan the code next to the Jam Maker below:

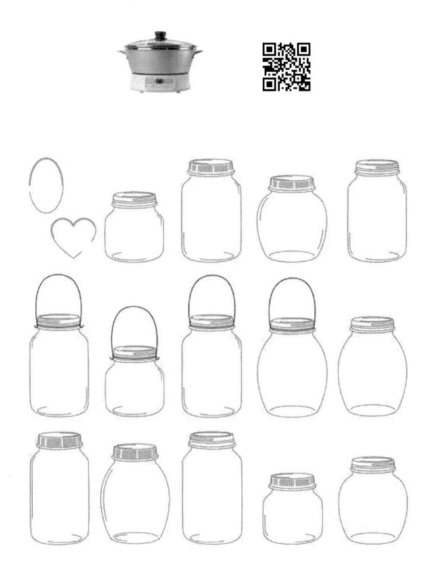

Printed in Great Britain
by Amazon

28395846R00073